God's Marvellous Jigsaw

The Story of Headlands Adventure Centre

By Michael Johnson

2015

INTRODUCTION

Over the years I have been asked many times to tell the Headlands Story, which I have done in several Churches and many times on Site. I have also been asked to write a book, so after many years and approaching the 30th Anniversary of the founding of the Site, I decided that this was a good time to do it.

This book is dedicated to my dear friends, Bill and Beryl Adams whose companionship and help gave me great pleasure, as we worked together over 20 years. So it was very sad for me when Beryl passed away but the last thing she asked me was how the hawthorn sapling trees that we had planted were doing, and was so pleased to hear that they were growing well and just coming into leaf.

Then two years later, Bill suddenly died whilst on holiday. He was with us at Headlands the Friday before he went away and was so full of life, that he made the cups of tea, and painted four windows in the games room, so it was a great shock to hear that he would not be coming back to us, but I have the fondest memories of them both and have missed them this summer.

I am sure that Beryl, having gone "Beyond the Gates" is enjoying the heavenly Paradise, and that Bill has his green paint and brushes ready in case there is any painting to be done!

I must also take this opportunity to thank my dear wife Cilla for all the times we have worked together at Headlands and also the time it has taken to type this book for me. So a "big thank you".

Remembering fondly:

Bill and Beryl Adams

Co-Founders and Trustees of Headlands Adventure Centre

Both were a great inspiration and still are to us and many others.

THE BEGINNING OF THINGS

Headlands Adventure Centre started many years ago, about the time of Noah in fact, when the gravel deposit was laid down in the Avon Valley after the Great Flood. The waters slowly drained away from the land, from as far as Salisbury Plain down the valley past Fordingbridge and Ringwood to Christchurch and out to the sea. But of course, there were no towns, villages or people. Gradually the land dried, people moved in and the earth became productive. Many years later, small amounts of gravel were taken from under the soil all the way up through the valley and then much more was taken from around Salisbury for the great cathedral church in 13th century. There were also small pits producing gravel for roads as people started to use carts, pulled by animals, and then the first of the larger quarries was started as towns became more populated and roads were required. But before this in around 1066 AD a king's hunting forest was created, so although very old, it is called the New Forest. This lies to the east of the Avon Valley.

In around 1920 the land which is now Headlands Adventure Centre and also the Business Park next door, was a small farm in the Parish of Ellingham, Harbridge and Ibsley in the village of Blashford, approximately 1 mile north of the market town of Ringwood. The land itself was probably used as grazing land and is bounded on the east side by the Lin Brook, a small river which rises on the Forest at Linford and flows into the River Avon and on to the sea at Christchurch.

In 1930 the land was sold/leased to a Civil Engineering and Gravel producing Company by the name of Hine Brothers. They extracted gravel from the fields which is now the Site and other fields around, namely the area between us and the Lin Brook and also the eastern side of the river creating a large lake known as Kingfisher.

The gravel was extracted from the ground by steam shovel and then by diesel excavators and transported to a washing and grading plant which was sited on the now Business Park. When the Kingfisher Lake was being created the gravel was transported over the Lin Brook and into the washing plant by a small railway. The parapets of the bridge over the river are still to be seen today.

Other Companies also started extracting gravel nearby. One was a Winchester based Company, known as A.J. Bull. They later became Hall and Co., then Hall Ham River Co., and finally RMC Aggregates. This was the largest producer of aggregates and concrete in the world, but they also had a depot at Blashford, which was finally taken down in 2007 when they became Cemex Ltd.

Meanwhile Hine Bros. were swallowed up by Amey Roadstone, who later became ARC. They were the last Company who took gravel from the area of Headlands Business Park and Kingfisher Lake. The Site was closed in approximately 1971 and left idle until 1982 when it was purchased by Avon Amenities Ltd, and the areas of quarry were filled in so that Headlands Business Park could be constructed. It was a building site for approximately 3 years until it was finished as we see it today.

Sometime back in the 1940s the Site that is now Headlands Adventure Centre was reinstated with the waste materials from the gravel workings and a large lake constructed that was known as Hurst Pond. Part of the restored area and approximately half the lake was sold to a Mr. Quigley, and a new boundary was constructed dividing the lake into two with a causeway and a fence, thus creating Hurst Pond and South Hurst pond as we see them today.

In 1983, I was working with a Company supplying sand and gravel etc., to the Construction and Civil Engineering industry, when a colleague (Chris Jones) and myself were made redundant. Chris decided to purchase the land and form a Company, Avon Amenities Ltd., to build the Business Park. He did have an interest in this land, as his wife is the daughter of one of the Hine brothers, who originally had the Site. As the Business Park construction continued, a small area (approximately half an acre to the east of the park beside the Lin Brook) was left as an open space, and the directors of the Company offered the use of this to the Bournemouth Battalion of the Boys' Brigade and the local Scouts, to be used as a camping/activity site.

At this time, I was the Captain of the 1st Tiptoe Boys' Brigade Company, so the proposal was looked into by myself and Nigel Galton (another of our BB Officers). We walked the Site on a very wet day with the weeds at shoulder height but decided that it was a good idea and would be a feasible project. A meeting of the Boys' Brigade and local Scouts was arranged. After a lot of discussion and "hot air" the idea was turned down by the Scouts as they already had several camp sites in the New Forest, and from the BB Battalion side that it would cost too much money (I think, too much hard work). The two of us from 1st Tiptoe decided to continue with this as a small Camp Site for the Boys of our Company, who were well pleased with the idea. We had always had a yearly camp at Marsh Farm, Rockbourne for many years.

So in 1987, the name Headlands Adventure Centre was born (named by the Boys), and this small area was cleared of weeds and brambles, mainly by the older Boys themselves, who spent a lot of time over there without any facilities, apart from the water of the Lin Brook. They named one particular stretch Washing Tackle Bay, but not only did they wash themselves there but also their pots and pans etc. The following 2 items were written by the Boys in their own Magazine:

> *February 1987 - A Work Day at Ringwood written by Richard Hillyar*
>
> *"On Sat 27th December, 5 members of the Company went to our camp site at Ringwood to help with some of the clearing work being done there. We arrived at about 1.15 and the first job that was done was the collecting of dead wood so that a fire could be made and so that we could cook our lunch. Andrew was the fire maker but because the wood was wet it was not easy to get it started so a quick trip was made to a nearby garage for a drop of petrol and then it was soon burning well. Meanwhile, David, Richard, Phil and Graham were clearing more dead wood away from the undergrowth at the far end of the Site for a future fire. Later Mr. J arrived with a lawn mower.*
>
> *Winter 1988 – Ringwood Weekend written by Michael Tomlin*
>
> *"We arrived on Friday 30th September at Ringwood. After we had put our bags in the caravan, we went down to the town to have some chips. In the evening we had a fire. It was quite tasty as a burnt offering. Paul and Roger had potatoes and a burned (Bernard?) Matthews meat pie"*

The land was fairly flat and level so the weeds, later to become grass, was mowed, and a fence constructed along the Lin Brook, so that now it could be used as a camping site. By then we had a water supply, laid on by the site owners, a portable toilet (nicknamed the Sentry Box or Pizza Hut) and a 35ft caravan given to us for accommodation for Junior Boys, while Company Section and Senior Boys used old army tents. Within 2 years the Site was used for a Summer Camp, weekend camps and an Open Day for Boys and their parents.

In 1987, our eldest son, Philip, who was also a BB Officer was moved with his work to Southend, where he joined the local 2nd Southend Company. The following year he rang to ask if he could bring some of the older Boys to Headlands for a Camp Weekend, so starting the use of the Site for Youth Camp Weekend Groups, other than ourselves. The following year, a second BB Company from

Southend came for a camp weekend, as did a Company from Altrincham.

In 1989, the then owner of Avon Amenities, (Mr. Richard Yonwin), contacted me to say that he had purchased the 6 acre site to the south of Headlands Business Park but as he could not obtain Planning Permission for houses, asked if we would like to use the area as an extension to Headlands Adventure Centre. After a quick walk through all the undergrowth, brambles, fallen trees (much worse than the original site), it was decided to say "yes we would like to take this on" and so the now Headlands Adventure Site of 6 acres is as you see it today.

SITE MAP 1985

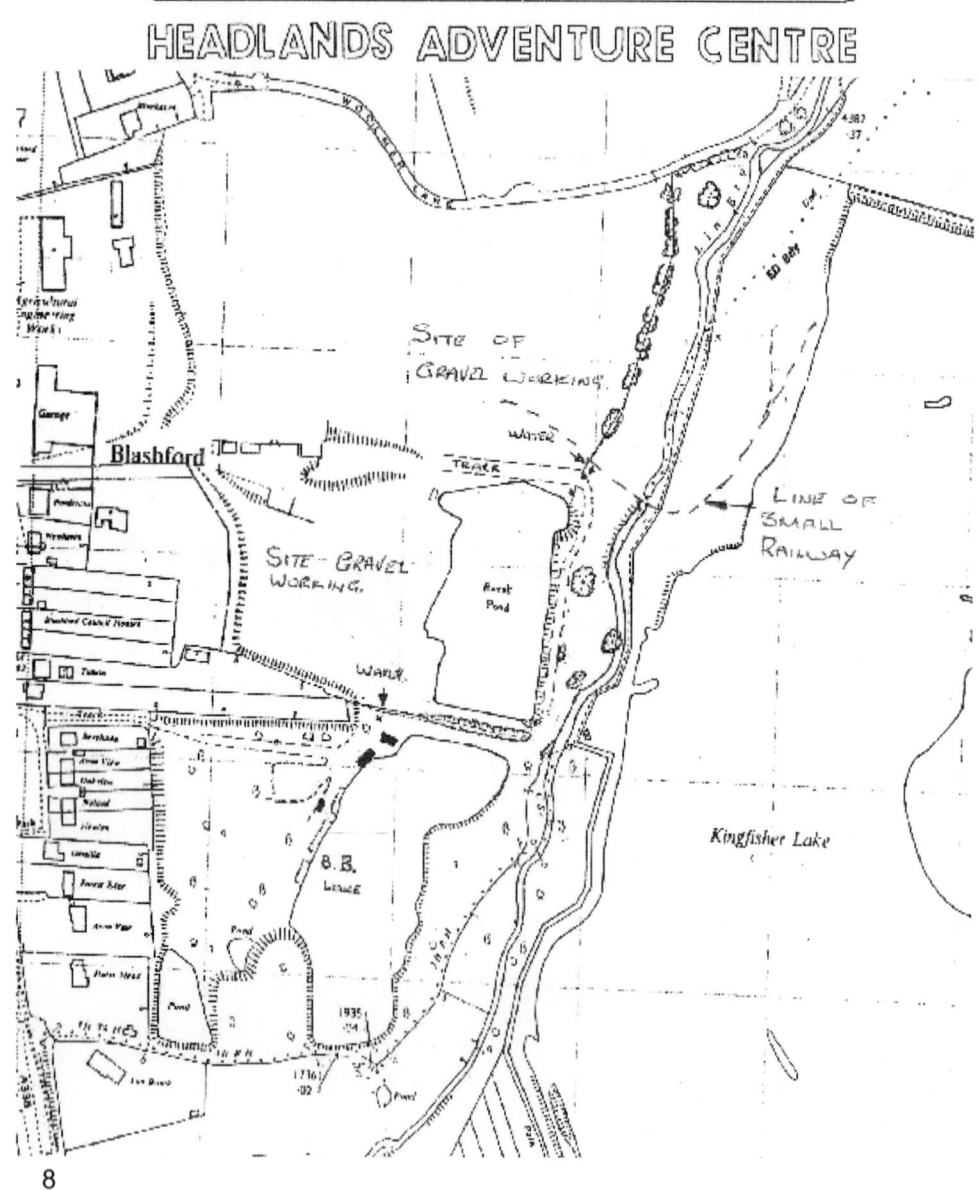

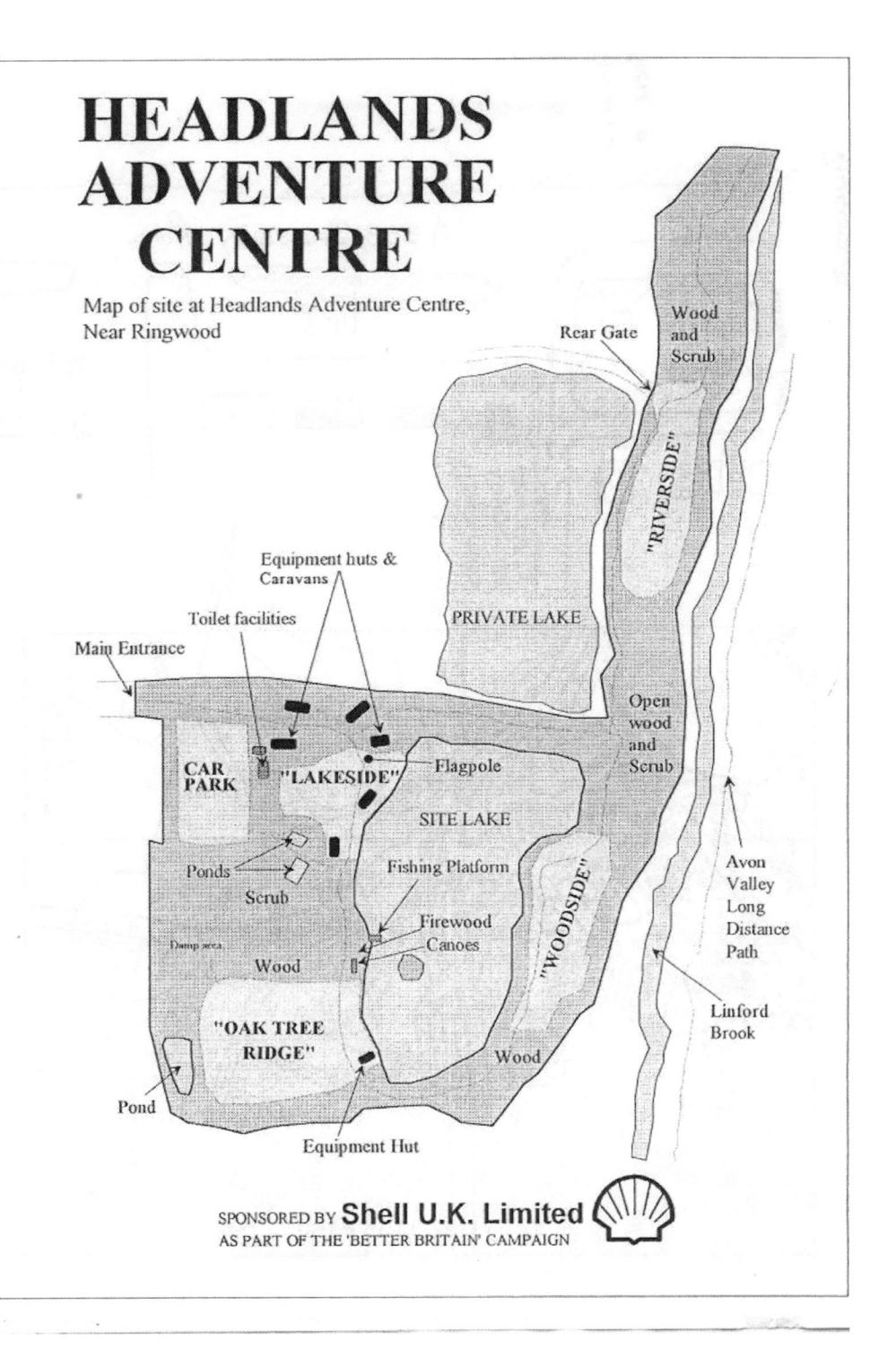

SITE MAP 1988

HEADLANDS ADVENTURE CENTRE

Map of site at Headlands Adventure Centre, Near Ringwood

- Rear Gate
- Wood and Scrub
- "RIVERSIDE"
- Equipment huts & Caravans
- Toilet facilities
- PRIVATE LAKE
- Main Entrance
- Open wood and Scrub
- CAR PARK
- "LAKESIDE"
- Flagpole
- SITE LAKE
- Ponds
- Scrub
- Fishing Platform
- Avon Valley Long Distance Path
- Damp area
- Firewood Canoes
- "WOODSIDE"
- Wood
- Linford Brook
- "OAK TREE RIDGE"
- Wood
- Pond
- Equipment Hut

SPONSORED BY **Shell U.K. Limited**
AS PART OF THE 'BETTER BRITAIN' CAMPAIGN

THE SHELL BETTER BRITAIN CAMPAIGN

1986

This certificate is awarded to the members of

1st Tiptoe Boys Brigade

in recognition of their contribution to the making of a Better Britain

Nature Conservancy Council   Civic Trust
British Trust for Conservation Volunteers
Shell U.K. Limited   Scottish Conservation Projects

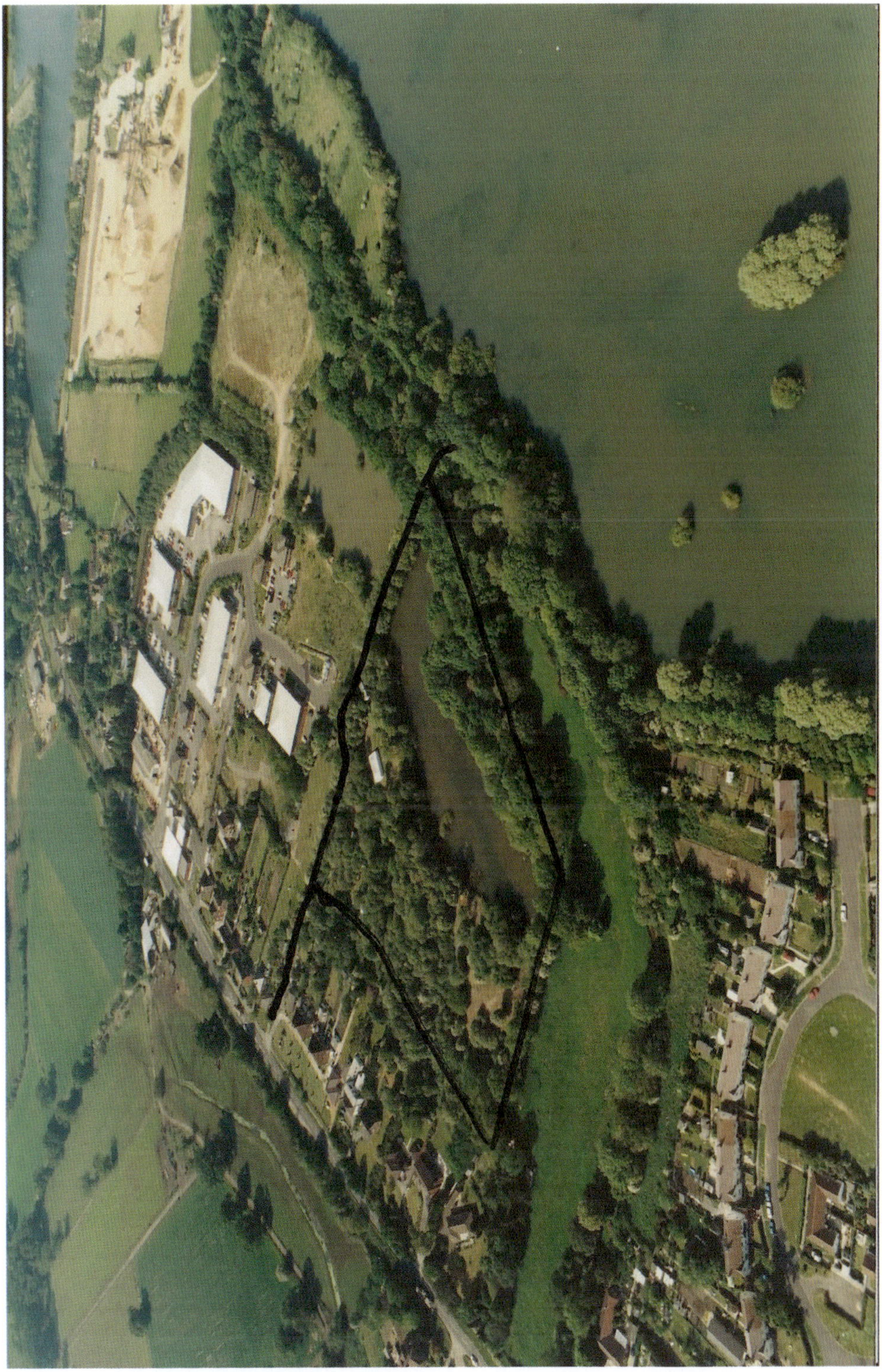

HINE BROS DIGGING GRAVEL AND THE PROCESSING PLANT THAT WAS ON THE BUSINESS PARK

12

**BRIDGE ABUTTMENT OVER LIN BROOK IN 2014 AND
LOADING GRAVEL ON TO RAILWAY**

13

1st TIPTOE WEEK END CAMP AND SUMMER CAMP

14

5th SOUTHEND BB SUMMER CAMP

15

CHAPTER 2

As already mentioned Mr. Richard Yonwin had offered us a larger area of land to the south west containing a lake which could be made available to us as an extension to the existing Camp Site, so a visit was arranged very quickly as this seemed a very exciting idea. The first thing we noticed was that the entrance was off the main A338 road between existing bungalows and not across the Business Park which was still a Building Site, and which we had been using. The second was that it had not been used for years; in fact, it turned out about 40 years. We very quickly agreed that it was the right thing to do on the same terms as the existing Site, and that it should be used for youth camping and outdoor activities, and that the owner could walk around whenever he wanted to. So, we set about making a small area usable after cutting off the lock at the front gate and clearing all the brambles away to make an entrance into the Site. The year 1990 was a significant one in the life of Headlands Adventure Centre in that we had the Boys of 1st Tiptoe on the new Site for a Camp Weekend. Whilst at Camp, we had a visit on the Saturday from the BB President and his wife from the Bournemouth Battalion to see that we were doing the job right. We did know Bill and Beryl Adams vaguely from seeing them at Centenary events in 1983. We now know that they were impressed with what they saw and the overall potential of what we had. The next year I had a phone call from Bill asking if he could put his caravan on the Site for a short time as he had been made redundant, and did not have a car to tow it or anywhere to store it, and if I could collect it from Ferndown. In the next day or two, the caravan was collected and taken to Blashford. We just about got it onto the small area that had been cleared, by the lake and near the summer house. It was agreed that Bill and Beryl could use their van and stay on the Site if they would kindly help us with some of the clearing. They immediately agreed to this and stayed on Site for quite a few days, and so began a long and very happy relationship with myself, Cilla, Bill, Beryl and Headlands. Bill and Beryl were going through a difficult time following the redundancy and often said how their early time at Headlands helped so much in the healing process and coming to terms with it. It was during this time that Beryl wrote the lovely poem that just summed it all up for her, and overtime it came to mean the same to lots of people. This poem is printed at the back of the book.

At this time in the life of Headlands Adventure Centre there were no plans to create anything other than a campsite for 1st Tiptoe BB. But looking back now in the year 2014, it seems as if God gave us a big jigsaw puzzle with hundreds of pieces but no picture on the box to go by.

As there were contractors working on HBP they were asked if the bank between the two sites could be removed and a gateway made. This was soon completed, and a gate erected. We then started to arrange monthly workdays – one Saturday a month – and many people have come along to help over the years. We began to clear the area between the lake, the summer house and Bill and Beryl's caravan to give us an area for camping. As we were clearing the brambles a shed was found just about ten feet in front of the present cookhouse, which we took down and used later as a store and will be finally demolished (but it still stands in 2014). Just before the main contractors finished on HBP, they gave us their two old caravans that were being used as offices. The roads into the business park were now finished so as Nigel had a 4x4 he moved the caravans, plus the original caravan onto the new Site during the Winter as we had had to wait for frosty conditions when the ground was hard. The 'vans were placed where the BBQ is now, where the cookhouse is and by the summer house. When we had weekend camps, the summer house was used as a cookhouse, store and anything else that was needed as this was the only accommodation until the caravans could be cleaned, painted and put to use. One was left as sleeping accommodation, the second was turned into a cookhouse, and the third we called the "lounge".

**THE CAMPING AREA
BEFORE CLEARING
AND 3 CARAVANS**

CLEARING THE FIRST AREAS

19

THE SHED FOUND IN
THE UNDERGROWTH

CHAPTER 3

In 1995, we had a big disappointment as our Church, Ashley Baptist, decided to finish with BB and start Youth Clubs. I regret to say that we lost a big percentage of our Boys and the Youth Clubs did not last very many months. At around this time, the Youth Group from Bill and Beryl's Church, Winton United Reformed, started to use the Site for weekends, as did 1st Ferndown BB, based at St. Mary's Ferndown, and a few of the members and leaders came to help with Site clearing. We had a shed given to us by one of our own BB Boy's Dads which we re-erected for their Site Headquarters and Store on an area by the side of the lake and adjacent to Oak Tree Ridge (Oak Tree Bay). They also brought in a touring caravan which they used for meals and accommodation as well as their tents. We had managed to clear this area before the main area of Oak Tree Ridge was cleared.

With the closure of 1st Tiptoe, we had to decide whether to finish or to carry on, but I don't really remember this as a problem. We had to carry on! As I said we did not have a plan to start and run a Youth Camp Site for Church Youth Groups, but I strongly believe that God did. I remember thinking "The Scouts have this type of Site", and also on a trip to Australia in 1988, we saw a group of about 12 youth camp sites all belonging to different Churches. So, with all this in mind the 4 of us decided to carry on to see if this was another piece of the jigsaw that would fit. In the same year, the Site Owner said that he would like to donate the Site to Headlands if we formed a Trust so we did, but unfortunately his Company went bankrupt, and the Business Park and our Site was taken over by a German Engineering Co. that are based on the Park (Eberspacher). We met up with the MD to be reassured that they had no use for our site and were quite happy for us to continue with the good work. At this time, we were also running fishing competitions for Bournemouth BB Battalion and a few local Churches that we called Dads and Lads Competition. The MD from Eberspacher presented the winners with their prizes.

The Bournemouth Battalion have never really used the Site for any events consistently. I only remember two November nights we had firework parties for the Junior Section, and the ladies were serving soup and hot dogs from one of our caravans that we had converted into a cookhouse. In 1995, we contacted a Christian Company (Stewardship Services) to set up our Trust Deed. At this time, we had a fifth member of the Administration Team – sounds good doesn't it? This was Muriel Grottick of Ashley Baptist Church, who was interested in the flora and fauna of the Site. She used to do activities with the Junior Boys' such as pond dipping, leaf and flower identifying etc. She produced our first brochure and the wording inside is still the same today, but she decided not to become a Trustee. As well as Cilla and myself, the founding Trustees were Bill and Beryl and so the Trust was formed on 12th September 1996 but as already mentioned, the land did not become ours.

OAK TREE RIDGE AS IT WAS BEING CLEARED

OAK TREE RIDGE IN USE

CHAPTER 4

As I have previously mentioned, I have worked in the Quarrying Industry where we used metal sea containers as offices and storage units. These were insulated and had windows cut into them, so this gave me the idea that they would be just right for our use, and so do away with the caravans. So, we started our search for 2 containers which did not take too long, as not far away is Southampton Docks where there are 100s of them. A look in Yellow Pages led us to Williams Shipping who had a depot on the outskirts of the Docks full of containers for hire and for sale. On contacting the correct person, we were offered 2 x 40 ft units, one with the doors at one end only, and the other had been modified as a sawdust store, but were told that this would probably not be suitable for our use, but if it was, we could have it cheap. When we looked at it, it was just right with doors at each end. It was also lined with plywood, which meant it was insulated. God knew what we wanted before we even asked! So, we went away to think about it as we needed £2000 for them to be purchased and delivered, and we did not have anywhere near this. So, we talked and prayed about this to see if it was the right thing to do. We came up with the idea of a Sponsored Walk to the Site in two parts – 1 from Winton URC (B and B's Church) and one from ABC (our Church). This was held on the first available Saturday with refreshments at the end prepared by Muriel and a friend from Ashley. In the meantime, we had been lent the money to purchase the containers and by the end of the Saturday we were able to pay the £2000 back. This really was the start of a long and wonderful time that God really did supply all our needs, confirming that we were doing the right thing, and putting HAC on the map for His use and the blessing of many people.

Another of God's provisions, which came through Winton URC Church camps was that other people offered their services to help us in the work, namely Andrew and Gwyneth Giles and Dave and Mary Martin. We have been so grateful to them over the years for all their help.

In the May of 1995, Planning Permission was sought for the containers. This was given (temporarily) in August of that year, also in 1998 and again in 2008. Permanent Planning Permission was sought in October 2009, which was granted in December of the same year. The base for the units was supplied by Tarmac Ltd., as Bill and Beryl had met the local manager at Ellingham Show, and he agreed to do this for us free of charge. With the units in place we decided to see if electricity could be supplied and as we had a pole on Site at the entrance near the bungalows, this was an easy job for Southern Electric. In fact, it was so easy that it was connected within one week of contacting their office and before we had paid for it. It was also decided to put a concrete path right around the units. This was again supplied by Tarmac Ltd. at a very cheap price. The concrete arrived in a mixer and the driver helped by pushing a barrow after training Beryl to use the controls on the mixer. After a period of time two of these paths became the floors for the canoe stores. God had provided us with a few more pieces to the puzzle.

At around this time, we had a Girls' Brigade Company for a weekend camp. While they were there, they had a small problem with our "crude" electrical supply. Fortunately, one of the Officers had her boyfriend (Graham Rowland) there as a helper who was a qualified electrician, so he fixed the problem. After this Graham became a permanent member of our maintenance team and rewired all our buildings and has maintained the supply as well as wiring all the additional buildings and the CCTV cameras as time has gone by.

In 1998 when we were thinking about permanent Planning Permission, two of the caravans were so badly damaged that we scrapped them, but the third was moved and converted into a cookhouse in the same area as the existing. Just before the containers were purchased it was decided to have a new toilet block as the old sheds that were being used were well and truly past their sell-by date. This was constructed locally for us from our design and would cost us about £1,000, so we started fund raising but a kind lady at Ashley Baptist Church heard about this and gave us the money to go ahead and purchase. This was used until 2010 when it was taken down and in 2011, re-erected to make a new storage unit for the Site garden tools etc, so that the old shed found in the bushes in 1994 could be dismantled completely, but as I write this in 2014, it still stands. In the same year, two new units were purchased and brought to the Site, but more of that later.

On a holiday trip to Scotland, we stayed at a Camp Site at Oban, which had metal container units as toilets and showers covered over with timber to look like a barn, so it seemed to us a good idea to do this with our two containers, but as we had many sheets of corrugated iron given to us, we erected a roof and sides over the containers. This also stopped water lying on the flat roofs. A few years later, a flexible PVC roof was made and fixed between the units to make a covered games and drying area.

DELIVERY OF CONTAINERS

27

CONTAINERS ON SITE

DELIVERY OF CONCRETE FOR PATH, WITH BERYL IN CHARGE OF THE MIXER

**WHAT A MESS!
BUT WE CAN
CLEAN IT UP!!**

FROM CARAVAN TO COOKHOUSE

THE END OF THE LOUNGE IS IN SIGHT

CHAPTER 5

When 1st Tiptoe closed down, the camping equipment was given to Headlands, so this had been in use each year. It consisted of a 30 x 20 ft ex-army brown marquee, 2 x 12 x 12ft ridge tents and a few old frame tents. One day, Bill spotted in the BB Gazette that a BB Company in Birmingham was getting rid of their tents. They were contacted and the tents were still available, most of them being good ridge tents, so a trip to Birmingham was arranged to collect them, and they were used until they fell apart. In 1995 a local Scout group from Hordle came for a weekend and they had new white, lightweight bell tents with a zip doorway, just what we needed. So, details were obtained and two tents were ordered. These have been used each year since and we have gradually increased this number up to 12. We also have 8 lightweight tents for weekends as these can be erected and taken down very quickly, and also if they get wet don't take so long to dry. We also purchased a 40 x 20ft white canvas marquee with a grant from New Forest District Council, which replaced the brown marquee. This was used until we purchased our existing PVC marquee, when it was given to another Christian Camp Site which is situated on the edge of the Forest at Tiptoe.

Over the years, we have met and got to know many kind and helpful people; one of whom is John Heath and his family, who live at the entrance to the Business Park and have a tent making and hiring company, and it was from them that we bought the large PVC marquee. They also made the flexible roof between the containers and they very kindly keep all our tents in good repair, as well as putting up and taking down the marquee each year. Over all these years, members of Bill and Beryl's and Mike and Cilla's families have been involved and helped in many ways. Many thanks to Ian and Olwen, Martin and Heather, Philip and Diane Adams; and Philip, Andrew and David Johnson, Ian and Catherine Bates, and of course all the boys of the Company Section from 1st Tiptoe who were there at the start.

As we progressed, we found we were getting very busy in the Summer, so in 2001 it was decided to see if we could find a more suitable cookhouse, as the old caravan was on its "last wheels". One of our helpers at the time (Mary) spotted an advert in the free adds for a unit which could be converted to our needs, so the number of the owner was telephoned on the Monday and a visit was arranged for the Tuesday night. But on the Monday night Cilla and I went to have a quick look as it was only about a mile from our home in the boatyard at Keyhaven. It looked good from the outside, just the right size including shutters on the windows, and it was portable. Bill and I met with the owner the next night, and he showed us the inside – just what we needed. Now the price! But he also told us that no one else had contacted him, and that the unit had to be off site by Saturday. In our minds this lowered the price. We were right, the price came down to what we could afford, so a deal was struck. The next problem was getting it moved by Saturday. Being in the quarry industry I again knew very kind local people. I now needed one of them to collect the unit from Keyhaven. He was a local owner driver working for New Milton Sand and Ballast Co. He was contacted and agreed to collect it on the Friday afternoon. It was loaded onto his trailer by the boatyard crane and was taken to the lorry park at NMSB all with the MD's (Michael Babcock) blessing. All we had to do now was to transfer it to Ringwood, but the articulated unit that was used, would not be able to get in and out of the Site. It was also the start of winter, so any truck going on Site would severely damage the ground. So, another driver who had a smaller truck with a crane behind the cab was asked if he would do this for us, which he kindly did within a week. Because of the wet surface, the unit was put down in the car park until a later date when the ground was much harder with a frost, when he moved it from the car park to its existing spot.

All these small details fitted into the jigsaw, and all free of charge. God was certainly helping us with the pieces. This unit had been used as an electronic workshop for boat radar and radios, so was fitted out with full electrics, and was painted inside a nice canary yellow, so all we had to do was fit kitchen units, which were duly purchased, and very kindly fitted by a member of Winton URC. With the purchase of two new Calor gas cookers and gifts of two fridge/freezers, the cookhouse was finished and ready for use.

The old cookhouse was now totally redundant and therefore was scrapped, and the steelwork cut up for scrap. At the same time as this was being done, the barbecue was erected by a joint effort of members from Ashley Baptist and Winton URC Churches.

In the summer of this year, we ran a BB Camp Craft course for new officers from Wokingham and Wareham. This started on the Friday with a fish and chip supper and a video about hill-walking. The new officers also had to put up their own tents. On the Saturday we were joined by Nigel and Jacquie Galton who had been with us way back in 1985. Nigel took the Camp Craft Section, and Jacquie the Worship section on the Sunday. We were also joined by Peter Henderson of Fireguard Services for fire safety and the use of extinguishers and by George Emerton from Ashley, on catering.

We have discovered that God has a wonderful way of moving people about to where He wants them, as has been the case with Peter and Wendy Cobbett, long-standing friends of Michael and Cilla (50 years!), who moved back into the area, and asked if they could have a "look" at the Site. What a silly thing to do!! Since then they have worked "their socks off" alongside us all.

OUR ORIGINAL TENTS FROM BIRMINGHAM AND TIPTOE

ON THE BACK OF THE PICTURE IT SAID 1st FERN-DOWN OFICER LISTENING TO FOOTBALL!!

TENTS USED ON CAMP CRAFT COURSE IN 1995

CHAPTER 6

Back in the 1990's 1st Ferndown BB were also involved with us and had a 12 x 12ft shed and a portable toilet down by the lake at Oak Tree Ridge. The shed was given to us by a local builder whose son (Tim Frowd) was in 1st Tiptoe Company. After a few years they also closed down and the shed was redundant. We decided to take it down and re-erect on the south side of one of the containers which was now being used as a store in the winter and games room in the summer. The wooden shed was then converted into a shower room as the two showers in the original toilet block were not a good idea; so, they were taken out and used as two extra toilet cubicles. An extension to the shower room was put on the following year as extra toilets and washroom, as was the old summer house by the lake.

Every 5 years we had to obtain temporary planning permission for the containers, but in 1998 we were told by NFDC that we had to apply for permanent planning permission or move them off the Site. I think that this was the most difficult and frustrating time, as NFDC staff were not the most helpful people to deal with. Suffice to say that God had other plans and we were put in touch with the local councillor through the local Parish Council who were on our side. He was also on the planning committee of NFDC and above all a Christian (Bill Dow). Within a few days he had arranged a visit to the Site by the Planning Officer, something I had been asking for, for nearly a year. The day arrived and I met the Officer with Councillor Bill. As this was in August, we also had Chesham BB camping on Site, so both Bill and the Officer could see the Site in full swing. The Planning Officer was most surprised to find out that I had had so much trouble with the planning staff at the council offices (where have you heard that before?). Anyway, he was most helpful and liked what he saw. He was there simply to advise us on what we would need to change or add to the container units to make them acceptable for a permanent planning application, remembering of course that we had a PVC roof between the two. You've guessed it, the only thing he didn't like was the flexible roof between the containers, which had to be constructed with timber and covered with steel sheets. The external walls that we had covered with corrugated sheets and painted green he said that this was typical Forest construction! We were able to agree to his recommendations and to submit the final application within the month, and by the end of the year given permanent planning permission for the total site, with only one planning condition to meet, which was that the project had to be started within 3 years, bearing in mind that the containers had now been on site for approximately 17 years. This condition we were able to fulfil! God had now supplied a very large piece of the puzzle, all we had to do was find the money, but again He had this under control. Councillor Bill told us of a national concrete company (Hanson Concrete Ltd.) who had a local charity with money in the bank for organisations such as ours, so contact was made, application forms filled in, one or two telephone calls, and the money was supplied into the bank with enough to construct the roof, covering the whole complex of showers and washroom and a false roof over the cookhouse. We have been worried about this for several years as the cookhouse roof was flat and consequently held rainwater, so now we were able to construct a sloping roof so that the water would run off.

The main roof was constructed by Graham and one of his roofing friends, and the roofs of the cookhouse and summer house by Craig and Luke, two of Bill and Beryl's grandsons. By this time Mike and Cilla's grandchildren, Daniel and Charlotte, were also getting involved, and at the time of writing, we couldn't manage without them all. How wonderful that three generations have been, and still are, working with us.

After I had given a report on the Summer's activities at Milford Baptist Church, two of the members very generously bought us a ride-on mower, so we could replace the one built in the 1960s, as the cutter deck was worn out. However, the tractor unit itself is still used for odd jobs around the Site in the Winter. A few years later we were given a second-hand ride on mower which was so useful as it was taking 4 hours to mow the grass.

Hanson Concrete were thanked for their generous support for the roof project, and we were asked if we had any other projects in mind as there was more money available – if we didn't, we could soon find one! So, we decided to update the toilets and the waste system. Because the site is a disused gravel pit, there is no way that we can be connected to the mains, so we had to continue using the steel tanks, but on a larger scale. They are then pumped out by a tanker. We also decided to look for second-hand units with flushing toilets as opposed to the chemical toilets we had been using since the development of the Site. We got onto "our friend Google" and came up with lots of portable toilet units, all at the wrong price, some even containing music systems, but I don't think that BB Boys would appreciate that – the Girls' Brigade might! After a little more searching, we came up with 2 units in Devon on a Christian Retreat centre. I contacted the Estate Manager, who was working on behalf of the Lord Clifford, and arranged to go and see them. So, Bill and I set off first thing in the morning and arrived about 11.00 a.m. in the rain. The units were exactly right for what we needed with one or two modifications, as the ladies' unit contained a disabled section at one end, which we made into two extra cubicles. We also had to find two extra waste tanks to go under the toilet units, as flushing toilets meant extra capacity was required. Two days before our trip to Devon we found two such tanks just down the road at Bournemouth Airport, and just next door a transport company who would not only deliver them, but also collect the toilet units from Devon and bring them up to Ringwood. So, this was arranged for a day in November 2010. The driver left at 6.00 a.m. and was back with us at Headlands for his lunch. The vehicle was equipped with a crane, so the toilets were offloaded into the car park. Whilst having his lunch, the driver told us that he had also been in the BB "up North", and he had also worked on a youth camp site in Scotland. After another cup of tea, he went down to Bournemouth Airport, collected the tanks and delivered those also into the car park. Now all we had to do was take down the existing toilet block, dig out the area for the tanks, move the new units into place, level up, connect up water and waste system, connect to electricity and paint the outside, all by May!! It was now that our needs were met yet again, with extra help in Mike Warren, Ron Bates (Ian's father), Ted Bywater (whose daughter is Captain of Chesham BB) and John Lawrence (Wendy's brother).

ON THE LEFT OUR FIRST MOWER USED BY PAUL TOMLIN BB MEMBER

ON THE RIGHT MY DAD WITH THE FIRST RIDE ON MOWER

ON THE LEFT AND BELOW THE MOWERS GIVEN TO US AND STILL IN USE. THE LOWER LEFT A 1970 REBUILD AND STILL IN USE TODAY

1st FERNDOWN IN CAMP AT OAK TREE RIDGE

41

THE OLD AND NEW ROOF OVER THE COURTYARD AREA

THE COURT YARD AREA IN USE AS A DRYING AREA

OR AS AN EATING AREA

THE NEW TOILET UNITS ON SITE IN DEVON AND ARRIVING AT RINGWOOD

CHAPTER 7

On Monday 2nd February 2011, 4 of us, Peter, Mike, Ron and myself started work to take down the existing toilets and put the new ones in place. We had hired a digger and dumper for the week and by lunchtime we had taken down the old building and stacked ready to reuse at a later date. We had also dug up the concrete floor and roughly shaped the hole for the new tanks that would go under the toilet units. After a break for lunch it was off again to enlarge the hole for the tanks. We also dug out a new soak away and trenches for the water from the sinks and showers. The gravel arrived the next day, so the trenches and the tank areas had a bed of gravel put all over them ready for the tanks and the pipes. I have also said before that Companies and individuals which have no interest in Headlands, will help out if asked. On the Business Park there is a company named Merlo, who hire and supply large tele-handling equipment, so I went round and asked if they could lift the tanks and units into place for us. They readily agreed to this, with the first lift of the tanks the next day at 12.00 midday. So next day all preparation was done by noon and in came the machine and by 1.00 the tanks were in place, so a celebratory cup of tea was called for. After a quick lunch, we were off again to fill in around the tanks with gravel and put the pipework in the trenches. Once this was completed 8 concrete block piers were put in place for siting the toilet units on the next day. The larger gravel was delivered for the soakaway, which was tipped directly into the hole. Also, during the afternoon, we had a shower of rain, (the only one for the whole fortnight) so by the end of the day the Site around the toilets and in the car park was like a battlefield.

Wednesday dawned dry. The soil and gravel was compacted ready for the units to be lifted at 12.00 noon, when the machine arrived and completed the job by 1.00. So, the afternoon was used cleaning up the car park and moving all the excess material into the wooded area. During the next day, we finished this operation and also laid all the pipework in place. Friday came as another dry day and thankfully the area had dried up. We had a final clean up and washed the machines off as they were to be picked up later in the afternoon, and so we came to the end of our first week, thankful that everything had gone according to plan.

After two very welcome days of rest, we started again. This time Bill was with us, as were his green paint pot and brushes. While he worked on the outside of the units, others of us got to work on the inside. At this point we decided to replace the flushing units with new so a friend, Ken Davies from Milford Baptist Church, who worked for a plumbing supplier, offered to purchase these for us using his discount. So, we gratefully accepted. Since then he has joined us on our maintenance team. As the female toilet had a disabled area, this was taken out in order to construct two extra cubicles using the inside walls and doors of the old unit. The wastewater pipes had to be realigned and changed dramatically to flow into the underground tanks. Over the next week, the final siting of water pipe, waste pipe and electric cables was completed and ready for the units to be connected to electricity. Just before the camping season started, Graham installed all the lights and power, so the units were ready for campers. The first group to use these at the end of May was 1st Guildford Boys' Brigade, who were more than delighted with the upgrade, as were all the subsequent groups. The expression often heard was "thank goodness, no more buckets".

During the next winter, Bill and Beryl, Cilla and myself were invited to Lincoln Road Chapel in Enfield to a special Commissioning Service as one of their young ladies, who had camped with us with their Youth Group, was joining London City Mission. After the service refreshments were served, I was approached by one of their young men (Bob) who was now a Youth Worker in another Church. He said he was a carpenter and had three friends who were willing to come and do any job we needed.

So, we agreed there and then to put a pitched roof over the toilets as these units had a flat roof, and in time could leak. A month or so later, and after purchasing the materials, the four lads arrived for three days work to construct and erect the roof. This was finished on time, so with a big thankyou fish and chip supper, they left for home.

God really has been working "overtime" supplying us with the finance and the manpower to carry out work.

TOILET AND TANK UNITS ON SITE FROM DEVON AND BOURENMOUTH ALL IN ONE DAY

THE OLD SHED TOILET UNITS. ONE OF THE SHEDS WENT TO DEVON AS A CHICKEN HOUSE

GETTING READY FOR THE TOILET UNITS TO BE PUT IN PLACE

DAY 2 OF THE TOILET PROJECT

IN GO THE TANKS BY THE END OF DAY 2

**THEN THE PIPE
WORK
AND EXTRA TANK**

DAY 3 OF THE TOILET PROJECT

THE UNITS ARE LIFTED IN PLACE

52

STARTING TO BUILD THE TOILET ROOF

BUILDING THE TOILET ROOF

THE ROOF IN PLACE 3 DAYS LATER

CHAPTER 8

In the spring of 2006 a local civil engineering company, Raymond Brown Construction offered to fund and erect a new perimeter fence around two thirds of the Site where the existing fence was only a low strand of barbed wire, and was really of no use. This was gladly accepted, and a 6 ft chain link fence was erected with a new gateway at the rear between the old and new sites. Unfortunately, some of the local inhabitants did not approve of this, which they showed by cutting holes in it over the next two years. The police were not that interested in trying to find out who were the culprits, so it was decided to install CCTV cameras to see if this would stop or to catch who was doing this. That leads me on to the next chapter in our development. After we had completed the roof and toilet projects, funded by Hansons, we were asked if we had any more projects that needed money as they had some left, and if we applied, we would receive another grant. So, after a Trustees meeting we put together an application for a new small marquee, the materials needed for the CCTV cabling, 500 plants for a hawthorn hedge to go around the chain-link fence and a new gate at the main entrance. In 2011, this was accepted and the money gratefully received (God was supplying all our needs even before we need them).

After the Site was closed at the end of the season, the digger and dumper were hired again, and this time Wendy's brother John came along to drive the digger for us. A new trench was dug from the rear gate to the cabins and along to the cookhouse, in which was laid a new water main, and an electric cable to the summerhouse (now the Bunkhouse), and also the CCTV cables. By the end of the week, we had dug 220 metres of trench, laid 130 metres waterpipe, 80 metres of electric cable and 1500 metres of CCTV cable. We also back filled the trenches and levelled the areas ready for grassing ready for next year's camping. The pipework and cables could now be connected ready for use.

We also installed another wastewater tank in the car park to give us spare capacity in case the tanker which empties the main tanks was delayed a day or two. The new gates were also ordered and erected at the front entrance, and mighty fine they look.

In November of the same year, Peter and I hired a rotavator to prepare the ground all the way along the chain link fence, ready for the new saplings. A day or so later, Wendy, Cilla, Ron and I planted 500 hawthorns and blackthorns, complete with a cane and tube to prevent the animals eating them, and to date (Winter 2014) they are doing fine.

NEW FENCING

DAMAGED FENCING

TRENCHES FOR PIPE WORK AND CABLES

PETER ROTAVATING THE GROUND READY FOR SAPLINGS

PLANTING 500 SMALL SAPLINGS

CHAPTER 9

During a couple of wet years the rain affected one or two of the camps and the car parking area retained water for a long time, so when the camping was over, we again hired a digger, and John came once again to drive it. This time we dug a series of drainage ditches with a main trench running diagonally across the site to the small wooded area and then filled the trenches with large stone, hoping that this would act as an underground drain. This has worked very well with two ponds being formed in the woods.

Whilst we had the digger, we used it for other small jobs, such as removing large tree roots on Oak Tree Ridge. We also re-shaped the edge of the lake to create a small beach and making it easier to get in and out of canoes. This created a nice shallow area for small children, and for one of the camp weekends, it was noticed that they had put 10 or so green Tesco boxes upside down in the water creating an underground path so that when they told the story of Jesus walking on the water, the Headlands "Jesus" got out of the boat and walked to the shore. The same group, two or three years ago, had two Baptismal Services in roughly the same spot. This was Christchurch Baptist Church which is led by Rev. Chris Brockway, who in fact has the record for camping on the Site for the longest period of time as he first came when he was a member of the Youth Group at Winton United Reformed Church.

In the Winter of the same year, we reconstructed the old toilets on a concrete slab that we had laid in the summer (on the hottest day of the year!). The "Loo Store" as it is now known has electric lights (thanks again to Graham) and all the hand tools and wheelbarrows in their rightful place.

In 2013, yes, we had a lot more rain, and yes, the drainage does work in the car park. We then constructed the fence at the rear of the toilets, and a new post and rail fence between the car park and the rest of the Site. Wendy and Peter were able obtain 30 sapling trees from the Woodland Trust, and these have been planted to replace the ones that have fallen down over the years. As we came to the close of 2013, we again had very strong winds and a lot of rain. The level of the lake was very high and the whole Site very wet. We also had at least 11 trees blown down, some into the lake, so we knew what the work days were going to be like during the start of 2014.

So now with all the major works completed, the rest of the Winter will be used to do maintenance work and the usual cutting back of bushes and trees around the Site, as they grow out up to 3' each year, which means that we could lose this amount of space all around the edge of the camping area and in time the Site would be back to what it was 30 years ago.

Now as I come to the end of this record of those first 30 years of Headlands, we have just purchased and started to install new kitchen units in the cookhouse, thanks to Magnet Joinery who, yes you have guessed it, gave us a very large discount. Ron even found a carpenter from Ashley Baptist Church, Dave, who fitted the main units for us. We have also installed two new gas cookers – a far cry from just a double burner gas ring we started with all those years ago.

THE WINTER OF 2013/2014 WAS WET!

FROM TOILET TO STORE IN ONE DAY

CLEARING TREES FROM LAND AND WATER

TAKING OUT THE OLD COOKHOUSE UNITS

COLLECTING THE NEW KITCHEN

NEARLY FINISHED

CHAPTER 10

In our brochure, it states that the Site is rich in flora and fauna, so I thought you would like to see some photographs which I have taken over the years, showing this side of the site, especially on and around the lake. There are also photographs of the trees and flowers in bloom in the spring, and the berries and fungi in the autumn. The first lot of daffodils were planted many years ago by 1st Tiptoe Co. Junior Section to raise money for a missionary project overseas, and the bluebells have come up since we cleared the wooded area, and trees have subsequently fallen down, letting in the light.

Most of you that have camped have seen the carp and crayfish in the lake and heard and seen the kingfisher skimming from one end to the other. Frequent visitors are ducks, who, if they stay, give us great delight in their chicks. Occasionally during the winter we have visits from swans and geese, and quite often the heron pops in for his breakfast, even seabirds have found us out as an easy source of food, as we see common tern, cormorant and gulls.

During the night we also have visitors that have been picked up on our CCTV cameras, such as foxes, rabbits, and a badger who we spotted playing with a Frisbee! Occasionally deer visit us.

At one time Beryl listed the following that she had heard or seen whilst camping for a week:

Nightingale	Woodpeckers
Treecreeper	Owls
Jay	Bullfinch
Kingfisher	Heron
Coot	Moorhen
Nuthatch	Deer
Rabbits	Mole
Butterflies	Damselflies
Moths	Dragonflies

THE LAKE

TREES AND FLOWERS IN THE SPRING

LIFE ON OR IN THE LAKE

IS THIS CAMP SUPPER ???

COWSLIPS AND LILIES

A HOST OF GOLDEN DAFFODILS

Beyond the gate

Your peace is here Lord, calm and still
  It soothes the restless mind
It calms the spirit, heals the soul
  The world is left behind.

The mist lies low, above the lake,
  The grass is wet with dew
The air is filled with twittering birds,
  The sun comes shining through.

Kingfishers flash electric blue
  The grebe dives long and steep
Moorhens and coots chug quickly past
  And fish from waters leap.

A heron lands and stalks his prey
  Kingfishers sit and wait
Dragonflies of every hue
  All this beyond the gate.

'Peace, be still', the Master said
  'My peace I give to you'
How can we doubt, when all around
  His promises renew.

       Beryl Adams

CHAPTER 11

Over the past 30 years, the following groups have camped at Headlands either for weekends or for full weeklong summer camps. Some of these have only been once, others two or three times, and some are still regular visitors:

1st Tiptoe Com. & Jun. Sections BB
Christchurch Baptist Youth Group
Winton URC Youth Group (Fury)
Christchurch Elim Youth Group
5th Southend BB
Lincoln Rd. Chapel Youth Group
7th Southend BB
Upton Methodist Church
Altrincham BB
Canford Baptist Church
Ashley Baptist Church
Church of the Good Shepherd
2nd Sutton Coldfield BB
Andover BB
18th Sutton Coldfield BB
Andover Vineyard
Birmingham BB
New Milton Evangelical Church
Shoeburyness BB
Hordle C. of E.
Southampton BB
Milford & Everton C,of E. Youth
Eastleigh GB
Bournemouth Battalion BB
Brighton BB
1st Bournemouth BB
West Kent Battalion BB
1st Ferndown BB
Gloucester BB
Waterlooville GB
Shoreham GB
London City Mission
Croydon Youth Group
Hordle Scouts
1st Ringwood Scouts
3rd Ringwood Scouts
Westcliffe Baptist Youth

Huddersfield BB
Wigston GB
Chesham BB
Ryde BB
Guildford BB
Stubbington Baptist Youth
Woodley Baptist Youth
Northampton BB

BILL AND BERYL

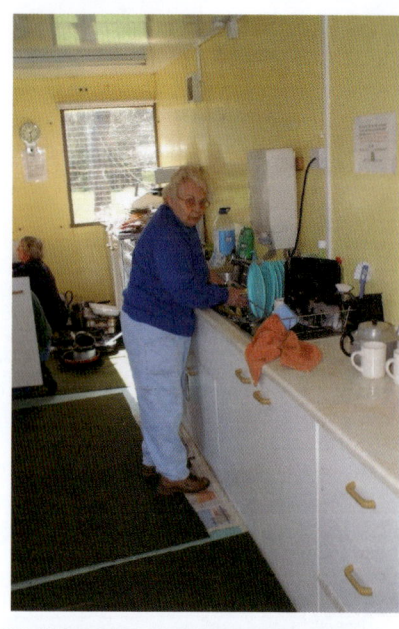

MEN IN THE COOKHOUSE IS THAT GOOD??

(RIGHT) A GROUP FROM GUILDFORD BB

DANIEL AND GRAMPS

A WORK TEAM STOP FOR TEA (AGAIN)

HEADLANDS TEAM WITH LOCAL MP AND HIS WIFE

THE WINTER WORK TEAM AT END 2014

CRAIG WAS NOT IN END OF 2014 PICTURE SO THIS IS HIM AGE ??? AND ALSO 2014

SITE IN USE WEEK ENDS AND SUMMER WEEK-LONG CAMPS

2nd SUTTON COLDFIED BB

CAMPERS HAVING FUN SUMMER 2014

5 th GLOUCESTER BB

CHRISTCHURCH BAPTIST MEMBERS GETTING WET AND ALSO FED

**WE ALL LOVE
A CAMP FIRE
AND A BBQ**

EPILOGUE

I hope through this little book, I have been able to show you how God has taken us on a journey over the last 30 years in setting up, financing, maintaining and administering Headlands Adventure Centre.

I am also indebted to all those individuals who have helped in this project in any way either on one occasion or over many years. Without your support this could never have been achieved.

You will notice from the pictures that there are not many of the actual camps that have taken place, showing the children, leaders and activities, as this is just a record of the history of the Site.

I must also mention the many Businesses that have helped us along the way, and some that still do on a regular basis, supplying us with finance, materials and services.

So, what of the future? Since the passing of Beryl and Bill, we have been able to appoint new younger Trustees, two of whom (to our joy) are the next generation of the Founders, namely Catherine Bates and Craig Adams.

The major development has been done, leaving us with the regular annual general maintenance so that we are able to continue welcoming campers each year as our Booking List is full. And so, the jigsaw pieces have fallen into place, but you will notice that on the front cover there are three empty spaces, so we are waiting to see with what or whom God will fill them.

FINALE: Found amongst Bill's jottings was the following:

> *"Coming home last night, Beryl said, 'I wonder if there will be a time when the only thing to do at Headlands is to cut the grass. I DOUBT IT!"*

79

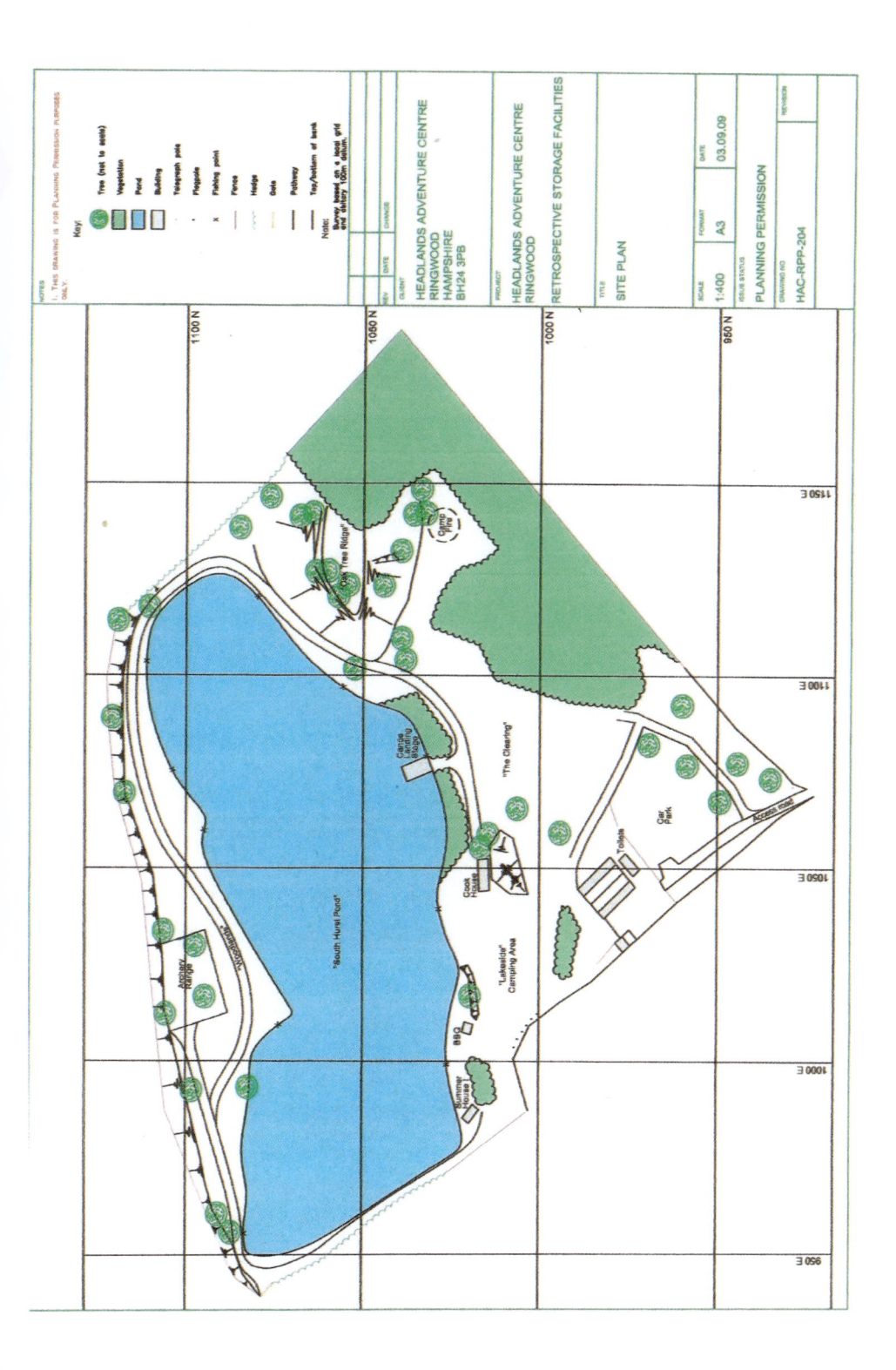

Printed in Great Britain
by Amazon